HOW DID THAT GET TO MY TABLE?

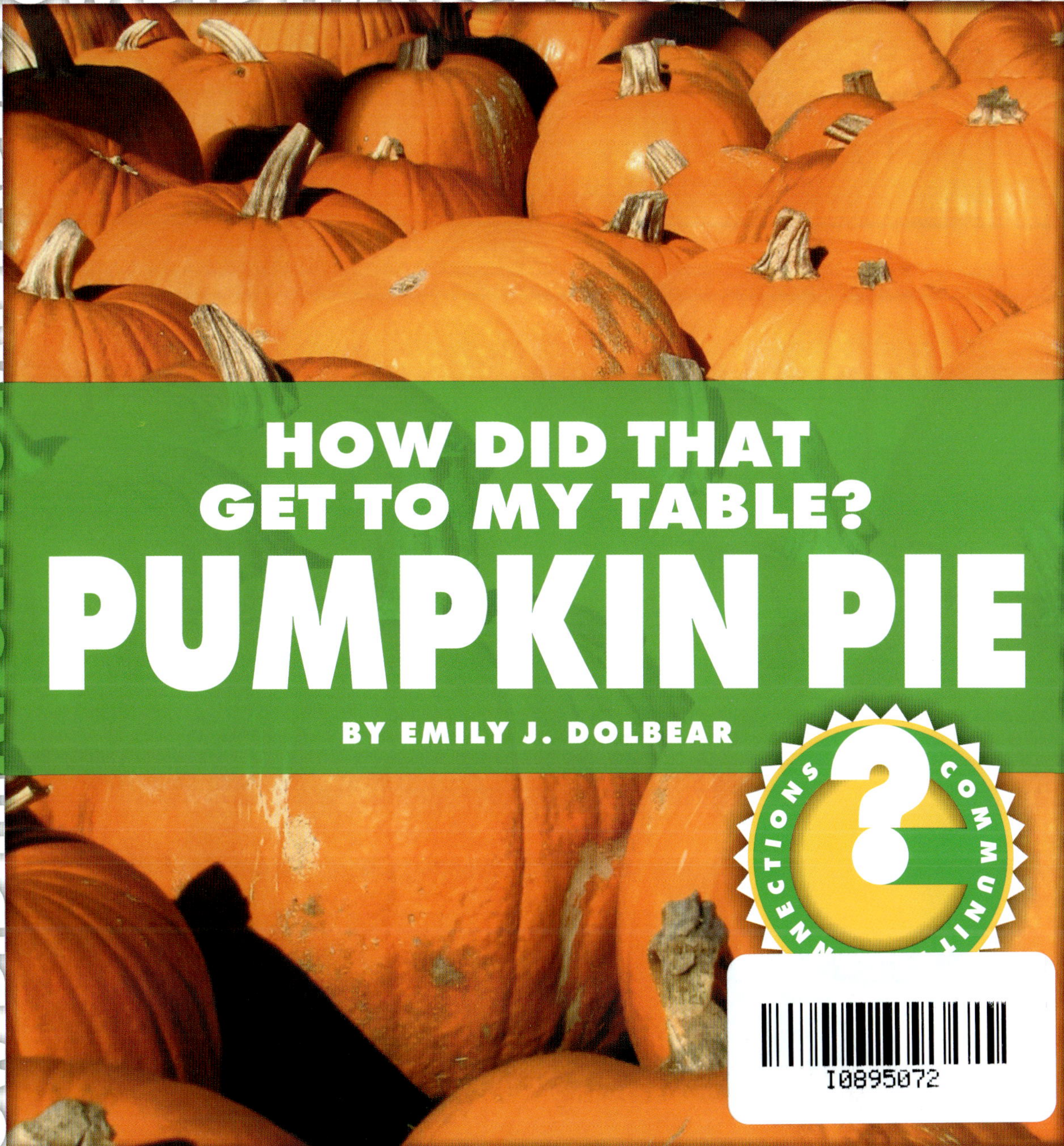

HOW DID THAT GET TO MY TABLE?

PUMPKIN PIE

BY EMILY J. DOLBEAR

COMMUNITY CONNECTIONS

PUMPKIN PIE

Published in the United States of America by Cherry Lake Publishing
Ann Arbor, Michigan
www.cherrylakepublishing.com

Content Advisers: Anuradha Prakash, PhD, Professor, Food Science, Chapman University
Reading Adviser: Cecilia Minden-Cupp, PhD, Literacy Consultant

Photo Credits: Cover and page 1, ©Erik E. Cardona, used under license from Shutterstock, Inc.; page 5, ©Lisa F. Young, used under license from Shutterstock, Inc.; pages 7 and 11, ©Elena Elisseeva, used under license from Shutterstock, Inc.; page 9, ©V1/Alamy; page 13, ©David R. Frazier Photolibrary, Inc./Alamy; page 15, ©PeterG, used under license from Shutterstock, Inc.; page 17, ©Dcwcreations/Dreamstime.com; page 19, ©David Wei/Alamy; page 21, ©Image Source Black/Alamy

LIBRARY OF CONGRESS CATALOGING-IN-PUBLICATION DATA
Dolbear, Emily J.
How Did That Get to My Table? Pumpkin pie / by Emily J. Dolbear.
p. cm.—(Community connections)
Includes index.
ISBN-13: 978-1-60279-472-6
ISBN-10: 1-60279-472-3
1. Pies—Juvenile literature. I. Title II. Series.
TX773.D638 2009
641.8'652—dc22 2008050640

Cherry Lake Publishing would like to acknowledge the work of The Partnership for 21st Century Skills. Please visit *www.21stcenturyskills.org* for more information.

CONTENTS

WHAT'S FOR DESSERT?

Thanksgiving dinner is over. You ate your turkey and mashed potatoes. You ate your vegetables. It's time for dessert. Many people like **pumpkin** pie with whipped cream! How did this yummy dessert get to your table? Let's find out.

Pumpkin pie is a tasty holiday treat.

GROWING ON VINES

All pumpkin pies start out as pumpkins. Pumpkins grow on vines along the ground. Pumpkins are round and orange. They usually weigh between 10 and 20 pounds (4.5 and 9 kilograms).

Pumpkins are very large fruits.

LOOK!

Did you know that pumpkins are not vegetables? They are **fruits**. That means they have seeds. Tomatoes and cucumbers are also fruits. Look for other fruits at the grocery store. How many can you find?

Farmers plant pumpkin seeds in groups called hills. The pumpkins need time to grow. They must be **harvested** before it gets too cold. Pumpkin plants will die if they freeze.

The harvested pumpkins are put onto trucks. The trucks take the pumpkins from the farm to a factory.

This truck has arrived at a factory. It is dumping its load of pumpkins into a container.

PUMPKINS AND PIE

What happens at the factory? Machines wash the pumpkins and cut them into small chunks. Then the pumpkins are steamed. The skins and seeds are removed. Other machines mash the soft pumpkin pieces. The pumpkin is now ready to make into pie.

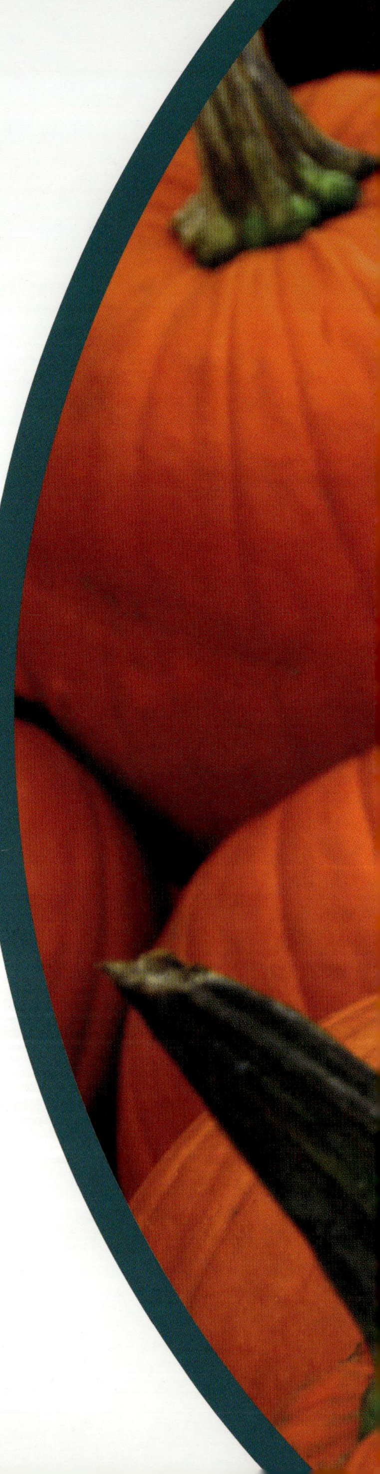

Factories turn pumpkins like these into yummy pie filling.

THINK!

Some kinds of pumpkins are very small. Other kinds can weigh more than 100 pounds (45 kg)! Most pumpkins sent to factories weigh about 20 pounds (9 kg). Very large or very small pumpkins are not sent to the factory. Why do you think this is so?

It is faster to make a pie at a factory than at home. Machines mix the **ingredients** for the pumpkin filling. Then they **knead** the dough. They roll and cut the dough for the crust. Another machine shoots the filling into the crust. The machine can fill as many as 100 pies a minute! Then the pies are baked in large ovens.

Pies have to be put in packages before they are shipped to stores.

For homemade pies, you have to knead the dough by hand. You have to roll and cut the dough by hand, too. To make the filling, you mix mashed pumpkin, milk, eggs, sugar, salt, and spices. Then you pour the filling into the crust and bake the pie.

Have you ever helped roll out dough for a pie?

MAKE A GUESS!

Did you know you can buy mashed pumpkin in cans? Many fruits and vegetables are canned at factories. Machines seal the lids. The cans are heated to a high **temperature**. Why do they heat the cans? Hint: Heat kills germs.

LET'S BUY A PIE!

Many people buy pumpkin pies for Thanksgiving. Pumpkins are harvested in the fall. That's why pumpkin pie is most popular this time of the year. You'll see pumpkin pies in many stores. How do the pies get to the stores?

Harvesting pumpkins can be a lot of fun!

Many local bakeries sell pies. They may also use trucks to take fresh pies to grocery stores. Look for them in the bakery section.

Large food companies often sell frozen pumpkin pies. They are shipped in freezer trucks. You will find those pies at the grocery store, too. They will be in the frozen food section.

You can buy fresh pies and other treats at a bakery.

Tartelette
Choco-framboises
Tartelette
Amandine et framboises
2,25 $
CHOCO-FRAMBOISE
TARTELETTE
Sucre
2,25$
FRAMBOISIER
MOKACCINO
OPERA
CHOCO-FRAMBOISE
Sucre
TARTE
Amandine
7,00$
TARTE
Choco-framboise
7,00$

Fresh or frozen, your pumpkin pie started out on a pumpkin farm. Now you know how pumpkin pies are made. It is time for dessert! Be sure to tell everyone what you know about how it got to your table.

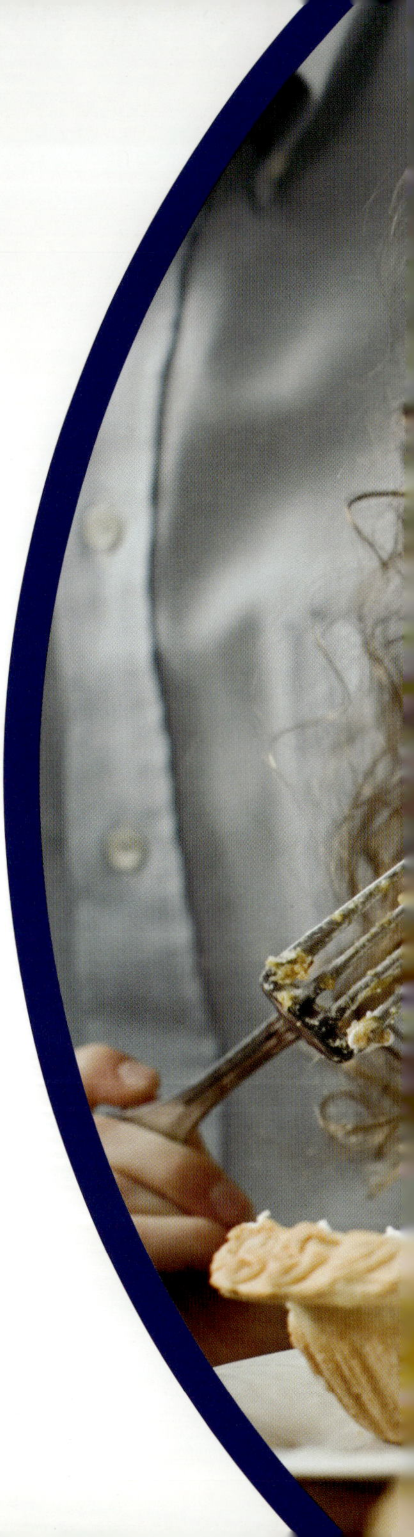

Dig in to a tasty piece of pumpkin pie!

ASK QUESTIONS!

Do you know someone who works in a bakery? Ask him or her where the bakery gets the pumpkin for its pies. How are the bakery's pies delivered to stores? Asking questions is a good way to find out how foods get to your table.

GLOSSARY

fruits (FROOTS) seed-bearing plant parts that are fleshy or juicy, often eaten as food

harvested (HAR-vest-ed) gathered up crops from a field

ingredients (in-GREE-dee-uhnts) the foods that make up a mixture or recipe

knead (NEED) to mix a dough by pressing, folding, and stretching it

pumpkin (PUHMP-kin) a large, round, usually orange fruit that grows on a vine along the ground

temperature (TEM-pur-uh-chur) a degree of hotness or coldness, usually measured with a thermometer

FIND OUT MORE

BOOKS

Gibbons, Gail. *The Vegetables We Eat.* New York: Holiday House, 2007.

Robbins, Ken. *Pumpkins.* New Milford, CT: Roaring Book Press, 2006.

WEB SITES

American Pie Council

www.piecouncil.org/press_room/index.php
Download some pie fun facts and information about the history of pie

Easy Pumpkin Pie Recipe

kidscooking.about.com/od/pies/r/easypumpkin-pie.htm
Ask an adult to help you make this pumpkin pie recipe

Pumpkins & More—Pumpkin Facts

www.urbanext.uiuc.edu/Pumpkins/facts.html
Read many interesting facts about pumpkins

INDEX

ABOUT THE AUTHOR

Emily J. Dolbear works as a freelance editor and writer of children's books. She lives with her husband and two sons in Brookline, Massachusetts. Her sister's favorite pie is pumpkin.